Watch Me Grow!

Christine Finochio • Jennette MacKenzie

"Look at my baby picture," said Marco.

"You have changed since the day you were born," said Pappa.

"You are growing to be a big boy," Pappa continued. "There are three things that help you to grow. They are food, exercise, and rest.

Your body needs food to grow," said Pappa. "Food is the fuel that gives your body energy. You need energy to play, work, and think."

"I understand," said Marco.
"A car needs gas to make it go. My body needs food to make it go!"
"That's right," said Pappa.

"You need to eat a healthy breakfast so your body has energy to start the day," said Pappa.

"I need to eat a good lunch and supper, too," said Marco. "Yes," said Pappa. "We all have to make sure we eat the right amounts of food, too. If we eat too much, we don't feel well. If we don't eat enough, we can't work.

We also need to exercise to keep our bodies working well," said Pappa.

"Running is good exercise," said Marco.

"So is jumping and skipping," replied Pappa.

"There are many ways we can get exercise. When we can, we should walk or ride our bikes.

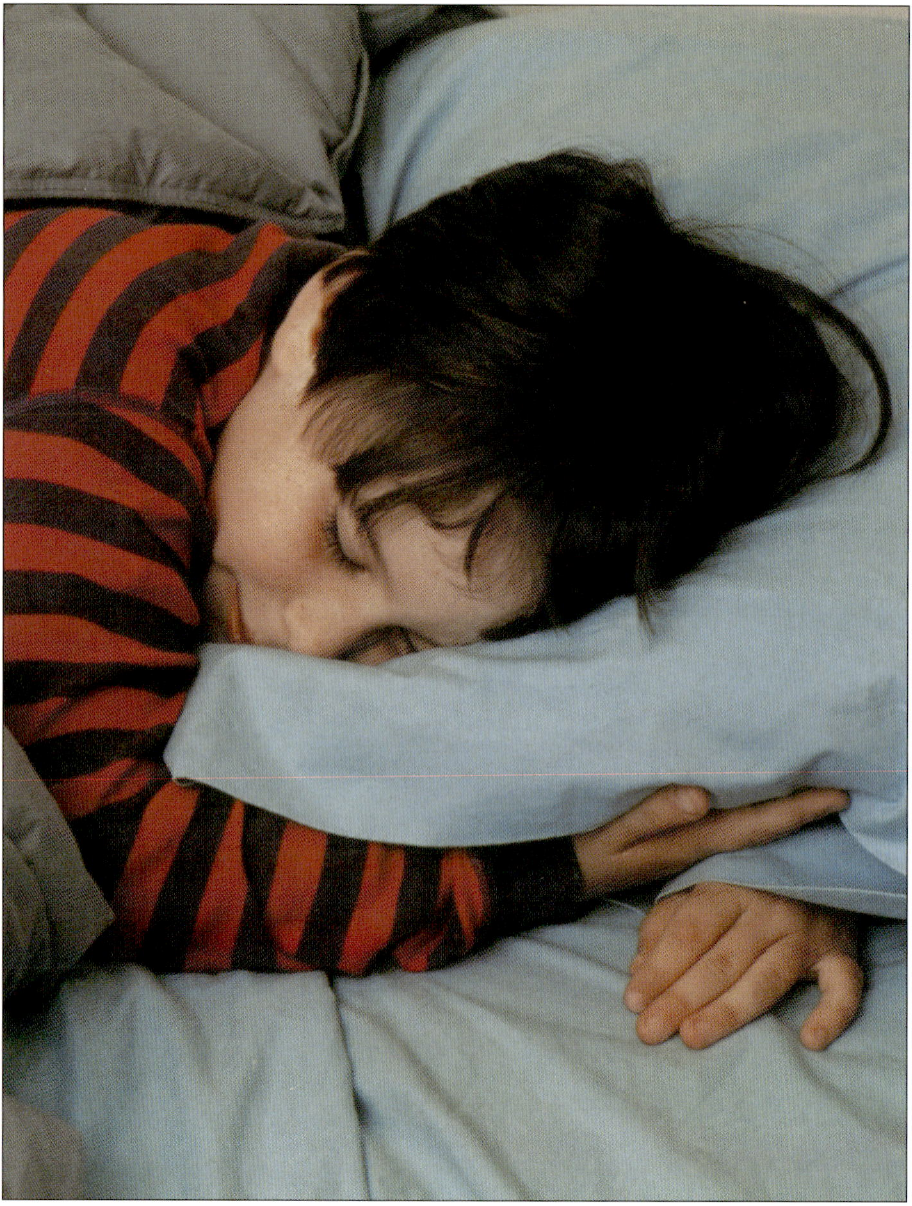

The third thing we need is rest," said Pappa. "Our bodies need time to rest. You need to sleep for eight to ten hours every night.

Sometimes you can rest without sleeping," said Pappa. "You can sit quietly or read a book.

You can watch TV or listen to music. These quiet activities help your body to rest.

"If you eat healthy foods, exercise, and get enough rest, you will grow to be big and strong," said Pappa.

"Will I be as big as you?" asked Marco.

Pappa smiled. "You may grow to be even bigger!"